THEN & NOW

THE
CRESCENTA VALLEY

OPPOSITE: In 1915, area photographer B. D. Jackson shot this panorama of the Crescenta Valley looking northeasterly from the Verdugo Mountains, depicting parts of what are now Glendale, Montrose, La Crescenta, and La Cañada. The orchards and vineyards show the agrarian origins, but there are hints of what is to come: the winding streets of Montrose lined with utility poles. Some of the buildings pictured here are still standing, notably the powerhouse for the Glendale and Montrose Railway, the barn now owned by Anawalt, and the Potts Building at the southwest corner of Honolulu Avenue and Verdugo Road. (Courtesy of the Glendale Public Library Archives.)

THEN & NOW

THE
CRESCENTA VALLEY

Robert Newcombe, Mike Lawler,
and the Historical Society
of the Crescenta Valley

Library of Congress Control Number: 2009942524

Published by Arcadia Publishing
Charleston SC, Chicago IL, Portsmouth NH, San Francisco CA

Printed in the United States of America

For all general information contact Arcadia Publishing at:
Telephone 843-853-2070
Fax 843-853-0044
E-mail sales@arcadiapublishing.com
For customer service and orders:
Toll-Free 1-888-313-2665

Visit us on the Internet at www.arcadiapublishing.com

ON THE FRONT COVER: These views are looking across the Crescenta Valley from the San Rafael Mountains, west toward the Verdugo Mountains. Verdugo Road and Honolulu Boulevard cut across the newly cleared sagebrush in this photograph taken in 1915, soon after the founding of Montrose. The commercial core of Montrose has blossomed today into a vibrant mix of old and new, offering residents the advantages of a small-town atmosphere located close to the conveniences of an urban Los Angeles. (Then photograph, courtesy of the Glendale Public Library Archives; now photograph, author's collection.)

ON THE BACK COVER: In 1914, developers Holmes and Walton extended the electric trolley line from Glendale into their new development of Montrose. The Glendale and Montrose Railway (G&M) played a pivotal role in the early growth of the Crescenta Valley in that it not only carried passengers but also freight, delivering supplies to the valley as well as hauling the valley's crops to Los Angeles. The Dinky is shown here in 1923 making a stop at the corner of Honolulu Boulevard and Verdugo Road. The G&M went out of business in 1930. (Courtesy of the Glendale Public Library Archives.)

CONTENTS

Acknowledgments

The then photographs in the book came from a variety of sources, including the County of Los Angeles Public Library, Glendale Public Library Archives, and the Historical Society of the Crescenta Valley. Other individuals and organizations that have contributed photographs to this collection include Ananda Ashrama, Frank Boyer, Lyle Draves, John Drayman, Betty Gjesdal, Katherine Halford, Mark Havlik, Maynard Hine, Fred Koegler, Mike Morgan, Patricia Nielson, Joe and Linda Rakasits, Mary Strauss, Jerry Weinberg, and Gene Zimmer. The now photographs were taken by Robert Newcombe and Mike Lawler.

We would like to thank our wives, Debbie and Pam, for putting up with the missed family gatherings and other messes a project like this creates.

Mike Lawler, in his role as president of the Historical Society of the Crescenta Valley, sends his appreciation to Robert Newcombe for donating his time and energy to this project. All profits from this book will be donated to the historical society.

A special word of thanks should go out to current residents of the Crescenta Valley, who have embraced and celebrated their history and heritage like few other communities in Greater Los Angeles. Their enthusiasm for projects like this is what makes the Crescenta Valley a great place to live.

INTRODUCTION

One of the problems with "Then and Now" books is that they almost immediately become "Then and Then." Even while gathering photographs and writing captions, changes were happening in the Crescenta Valley, virtually guaranteeing that some of the now photographs would be then by the time this book is published. The new library and Indian Springs Shopping Center are still under construction as the text is finished. New businesses have opened where others closed. And there are plans to demolish some buildings included here. To keep up-to-date, almost all of the now photographs were reshot within weeks of the deadline.

Almost every "now" photograph was shot at the same angle that the "then" photograph was shot, but that was not always possible, especially where vegetation has grown to block parts of the subject. For example, in Dunsmore Park, today there are large sycamore trees in between the folk art walls; when the then photograph was taken, there were no trees. And Montrose was all brick and cement in the early days, whereas now, the shopping park is filled with mature trees that make contrasting photographs difficult.

This book is not intended as a history of the Crescenta Valley but rather to show visually how the valley has grown and developed, for better or worse, in the last 140 or so years by contrasting old photographs with the same areas today. The book is broken up into four chapters (La Crescenta, Montrose, Glendale, and La Cañada), but it could just as easily be a single chapter, since the valley's history is tied together.

About a third of the "then" photographs show places that have completely changed, but most of them show buildings that still exist, at least in part. The amount of preserving, renovating, refurbishing, and just plain reusing of these old buildings that has taken place in the valley is a breath of fresh air in our disposable society, with local business owners being green years before it was trendy. The pairs of these photographs are perhaps more interesting than the pairs that show completely different landscapes where almost nothing is recognizable, like the canyon that was Indian Springs versus the shopping center and parking lot it is today.

The history of the Crescenta Valley is relatively recent, and much of it was photographed, so we are fortunate to have these photographs to share with you.

LA CRESCENTA

When Dr. Benjamin Briggs planned La Crescenta, he envisioned the intersection of Michigan Avenue (Foothill Boulevard) and Los Angeles Avenue (La Crescenta Avenue) as the town center. Shown here in 1895 is the southeastern corner, the site of the La Crescenta Store and Post Office. These two stagecoaches made regular runs to and from Pasadena, bringing guests to the resort hotels and lung sanitariums in the valley. The La Crescenta town center concept seemed to disappear for decades, but perhaps the new library will become one.

By the 1920s, the old wooden La Crescenta Store was replaced with this brick structure housing the La Crescenta Pharmacy. Later this was occupied by the iconic Spike Jones Market, a La Crescenta landmark through the 1950s and 1960s. However, like many brick buildings in the area, it was damaged significantly by the 1971 Sylmar earthquake and was torn down. More recently, it was replaced with this smaller retail center housing a florist and dry cleaner.

The Holly House was built in 1886 on the northwest corner opposite the post office. The Hollys came here from Illinois for the restorative climate. Holly, an engineer and inventor, constructed the eight-room home with indoor plumbing, including a hot water system, practically unheard of at the time. The house was torn down in 1962, replaced by a gas station. The new La Crescenta Library opened on this corner in early 2010.

Civil War veteran Theodore Pickens was the first American settler in the valley. In 1871, he homesteaded on land up against the mountains in the area now known as Briggs Terrace, and he built this cabin four years later. The oldest house in the valley still stands but not in the valley. In 1973, the Siems family donated it and its contents to the County Forestry Division, which moved the cabin intact to its Henninger Flats facility above Altadena.

Dr. Benjamin Briggs searched the world over for the perfect climate for the treatment of lung diseases and, in 1881, settled on Rancho La Cañada. He chose a spot high up the foothill to build his home-sanitarium, using cement he had imported from Germany. From this veranda, Briggs looked out over the valley and coined the name La Crescenta, inspired by the crescent shapes of the hills and valley below. The old cement home was bulldozed in the early1960s, replaced with a subdivision.

By 1890, the healthy climate of La Crescenta was attracting visitors, so a resort hotel was built on the corner of what is now Rosemont Avenue and Foothill Boulevard. At times it was called the La Crescenta Hotel and at other times the Silver Tree Inn, after an unusual silver-barked tree that grew on its grounds. By the mid-1920s, it ceased operation as a hotel and was purchased and used as a home by the Zimmer family. It was replaced by a mini-mall in the 1960s.

The Zimmers named their home Stoneleigh and operated a real estate office from a small building on Foothill Boulevard. Here Olive Zimmer sits by the fishpond, with the porch and front door of the grand old hotel in the background. The hotel was built entirely of redwood and had 32 rooms, including a separate wing with a kitchen and dining room. It was actually the second hotel on the site after the first one blew down in a fierce windstorm.

In this photograph from 1902, young Ray Bathey rides his bicycle down a Briggs Boulevard that is little more than a trail through an orchard. As the road was paved and widened, the steep incline has made speed a problem. In 2008, the Crescenta Valley Town Council was finally able to get a stop sign placed on Briggs Boulevard at Mountain Avenue, the first stop sign on that street in the 120 years since it was first carved out of the sagebrush.

This Victorian house and barn were built in the 1880s along what was then Michigan Avenue, one of several mansions near the new town center of La Crescenta. In 1923, Merritt Kimball bought the mansion and expanded it into Kimball's Sanitarium, one of the valley's few sanitariums for the insane. Locals fought further expansion, uncomfortable with the valley's growing reputation as "the place where the nuts are." Torn down in the early 1960s, the sanitarium was replaced by a shopping center.

In the 1910s, as more people moved to the valley, the runoff water from Pickens Canyon was not enough, so miners tunneled hundreds of feet into the mountain to reach the water-bearing fissures that fed the springs. While the miners used some dynamite, most of the work was done with picks and shovels. These horizontal wells were dug in many areas of the San Gabriel Mountains and still supply water to the valley. The photographs are of the Pickens Tunnel: right, today; below, during construction.

Bonetto's Feed was a landmark in the Crescenta Valley for almost 50 years. Brothers Tom and Bart Bonetto opened this feed and fuel store at the intersection of Montrose and La Crescenta Avenues in 1923 and ran it until they retired in 1971. It was a single-story, patterned brick building with a storage barn behind it for hay bales and feed sacks. The store was torn down and replaced with apartments, but the Bonetto House, a Glendale Historical Landmark, still stands a few blocks away.

In 1924, "Pappy" Bane opened the La Crescenta Pharmacy on the northeast corner of Montrose Avenue and Los Angeles Avenue (now La Crescenta Avenue). Pharmacies were the convenience stores of their day, located at most major intersections and selling a wide variety of goods and services. The 7-Eleven has been on this corner for almost 40 years.

The 1920s were a time of phenomenal growth in the Crescenta Valley. Constructed around 1925 on Foothill Boulevard between La Crescenta and Ramsdell Avenues, the Johnson Building became the new retail center of La Crescenta with the establishment of a post office, grocery, and hardware store. Still standing on the south side of the 2900 block of Foothill Boulevard, these buildings host a variety of retail outlets and offices, anchored on the west side by the long-playing Pedrini Music.

Johnson Building

In the early 1920s, the Crescenta Valley was home to world famous artist S. Seymour Thomas. When told of hopes for a new church, Thomas set up his easel on the corner across from the empty lot and painted his vision of the perfect chapel for the Crescenta Valley. He brought the painting, still wet, to the church design meeting, where all enthusiastically approved. The church was built from this design and looks nearly the same today.

This was Fire Station 19 when it opened on Foothill Boulevard between Rosemont and Briggs Avenues in 1930. It was constructed of natural stone to match its neighbor, St. Luke's Episcopal Church. When the department outgrew the small station, Los Angeles County sold the building to St. Luke's and moved the department to a new facility at 1729 West Foothill Boulevard in La Cañada. St Luke's uses the building for community groups, such as the Boy Scouts.

In 1923, Swami Paramananda, a spiritual leader from India and teacher of the Vedanta philosophy (a Hindu derivative that honors all religions), purchased the 135-acre Fusenot Ranch at the top of Pennsylvania Avenue and established the Ananda Ashrama. These beautiful gates, built at the entryway in the 1920s, welcomed visitors to the grounds for years, and still do, minus the arch.

In 1928, Swami Paramananda and church members began an ambitious building plan. The church compound, with three buildings and arched connecting walkways, was to be the centerpiece of the 120-acre religious retreat. In this photograph, the main church structure is taking shape as the church leaders pose amidst the construction. Eighty years later, the Temple of the Universal Spirit is one of the valley's architectural treasures. The church welcomes visitors of all faiths to their services.

The first school in the valley was established on Foothill Boulevard near La Crescenta Boulevard in 1887, but the area's population quickly outgrew it. In 1890, a son-in-law of Dr. Briggs donated land, and this steepled, one-room schoolhouse was built. When La Crescenta School opened that year, the bell in the steeple could be heard throughout the valley. The school started with 29 students; the largest enrollment was 40 students in multiple grades, taught by only one teacher.

The one-room school served the valley until 1914, when this larger school (above) was built on the same site on La Crescenta Avenue. It was damaged by the 1933 Long Beach earthquake and could not meet the building standards enacted after that disaster. The current La Crescenta Elementary School was built in the same location in 1950. In 1976, the bell from the old school was found, restored, and hung out front—it is rung once every year in June by the graduating sixth-graders.

Built in 1932, La Crescenta Junior High School was renamed Anderson W. Clark Junior High in 1938 after the death of "Andy" Clark, a local minister who had dedicated his life in retirement to helping needy local residents. In 1962, the junior high became Crescenta Valley High School, and the Clark name was passed on to a new junior high. The old school has been considerably added on to over the years, but the original structure still stands at the core.

Holy Redeemer Church was built in 1927 in a Mission Revival style at the corner of Montrose Avenue and Del Mar Road. The church managed to survive the New Year's Flood of 1934 (while walls of mud and water carried houses past it) and the construction of the 210 Freeway, but it could not withstand dry rot and termites. In the 2000s, the church was almost completely demolished and rebuilt to look the same.

The German American League bought a large, oak-studded park at the base of the Verdugos in the 1930s. When German president Paul von Hindenburg died in 1934, the park was named for him, and a huge bust (5 feet from chin to forehead) was erected. After World War II, the giant statue of the German leader went over like a lead dirigible and was repeatedly vandalized until the county removed it after buying the park in 1957.

The league sponsored German-themed cultural events and parties nearly every weekend. Attracting thousands, these celebrations featured oompah bands, kegs of beer, and elaborate outdoor stage events. The first Oktoberfest ever held in California took place here in 1956. In the then photograph, costumed performers pose by the wine stand. While the Hindenburg statue is long gone, the hexagonal base of this wine stand and oddly shaped cement pads of other buildings are still scattered around Crescenta Valley Park.

This Shopping Bag was the first large supermarket to open on Foothill Boulevard, built around 1950 to serve the growing postwar population of the valley. This Shopping Bag was unique in that it featured not only a coffee shop but also, on the lower level, a department store and garden shop. This building has been home to several different markets. In the 1990s, the current tenant, Orchard Supply Hardware, moved in and put its garden center on the lower level.

Pete and Link Paola bought the Williamson Oldsmobile dealership at Foothill Boulevard and Glenwood Avenue in 1951. They soon added this stylish showroom next door at 2865 Foothill Boulevard. The Paola Oldsmobile showroom is shown here in late 1956, with the new 1957 models just in. Paola Oldsmobile left this location in the mid-1960s. The building is now home to the Antique Store.

In 1948, La Crescenta Frozen Food Lockers offered on-site butchering services and freezers to store large quantities of meat. At the time, this was still a rural community, and it was not unusual for local hunters to bag a deer in the mountains or for residents to raise livestock for the table. In the same location, Harmony Farms sells naturally grown beef and poultry as well as ostrich and elk. And they still have the frozen food lockers for rent.

In August 1949, the Hine family is laying the subfloor in a unit of their new motel, the May Lane. From left to right are Glen Hine and his two teenaged kids, Maynard (May) and Alane (Lane). The family ran the May Lane until the early 2000s, when they sold it to a developer. There have been several proposed developments for the site, but for now it hosts a pumpkin patch, Christmas tree lot, and occasional film shoot.

This charming, barn-style house, built in the 1920s, stood at the southwest corner of Rosemont Avenue and Foothill Boulevard for nearly 80 years, owned by only a few families. In the 1980s, the house served as an antique store, but it was abandoned in the 1990s and torn down in 2001. The imposing, cold-looking office building that replaced it galvanized the community and led to the creation of the Foothill Design Committee and the Foothill Boulevard Design Guidelines.

MONTROSE

Around 1910, developers Holmes and Walton bought the southeast portion of the Crescenta Valley, named it Montrose, and laid out the streets in a rose pattern. On February 22, 1913, they hosted a huge barbecue that attracted close to 4,000 potential buyers. In this photograph, the barbecue is in the middle left; the future Sparr Heights is the fruit orchards above; the future Montrose business district is in the center; and the future Indian Springs site is the oak grove in the lower right.

In 1914, this building on the southwest corner of Honolulu Avenue and Verdugo Road was the first commercial building in Montrose. It was leased by the Potts family and became the Montrose Hardware and Grocery Store. They also dispensed gasoline from a pump out on the curb. This building has been occupied by many different businesses over the years and is shown here in 1923 as a bank. The distinctive configuration of the building, with its curved front and stepped roofline, remains mostly unchanged.

Built in April 1913, the powerhouse for the Glendale and Montrose Railway contained massive generators that supplied the 600 volts needed for the electric trolley line. Acquired second-hand from Pacific Electric, the generators weighed 30 tons, and it took a wagon pulled by a team of 14 horses and 12 mules two days to move the generators up the Verdugo canyon from Glendale. This building near the northeast corner of Verdugo Road and Honolulu Avenue still stands, making it the oldest building in Montrose.

In 1923, the Dinky trolley of the Glendale and Montrose Railway drops off passengers at the intersection of Verdugo Road and Honolulu Avenue. The Dinky was smaller than other rail cars, with only one set of double wheels centered under the car, making a ride on the uneven tracks feel like a trip at sea. Here is the same view today, the entrance to the Montrose Shopping Park. The building under construction in the then photograph is now the Rocky Cola Café.

Built in 1923 by 21-year-old Joe Belanger, this structure was one of the first built in the valley building boom that lasted until the Great Depression. The Montrose Pharmacy, with its soda fountain and grill, at the key intersection of Honolulu Avenue and Verdugo Road, was an instant success. The Rocky Cola Café, a veritable icon of the charm of Montrose, occupies this building today, with plywood and stucco covering the original architectural details.

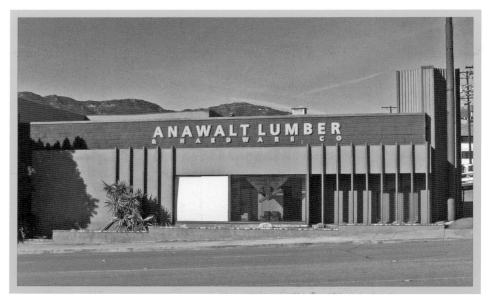

Anawalt Lumber opened in 1920, just in time for the building boom. The first store was located on Verdugo Road next to the Glendale and Montrose Railway carbarn and sidings. When G&M went out of business in 1930, Anawalt's bought the property and built a new store where the rail sidings had been. Shown below is the store in the 1950s. The building has since been remodeled—the entrance is no longer on Verdugo Road, but the elephant logo survives.

Here are the Glendale and Montrose Railway carbarn, trolley, and rail sidings in 1923. The G&M, an electric trolley, served the valley from around 1914 to 1930. Starting at Pennsylvania Avenue, the tracks ran down the center of Montrose Avenue and continued on Verdugo Road into Glendale. Anawalt's has used the barn for lumber storage since 1930. The barn still stands, and in the right light, the rails and ties under the asphalt are visible at the opening of the barn.

The Reinhardt Building on Honolulu Avenue, half a block west of Montrose Avenue, was the first two-story structure in Montrose. Built in the 1920s, it was constructed of bricks, typical of business buildings of that era. One of the unfortunate aftershocks of the 1971 Sylmar earthquake was that most brick buildings in Montrose were covered with stucco to stabilize them. The interior bricks have been exposed inside the current first floor occupant, the Black Cow Café.

The Montrose Hotel was built on Honolulu Avenue in the early 1920s as a residential hotel, with businesses on the ground floor and 15 rooms on the second, surrounding an atrium. Vaudevillians who performed at the Montrose Theater next door stayed at the hotel. It went out of business in the 1950s, and the 1971 Sylmar quake did enough damage to the building that the second story was removed. The first story remains and is home to Andersen's Pet Shop.

The Montrose Theater was built in 1924 by Stephen Meyers as a silent film and vaudeville theater, with a stage where live acts performed between movies. The carbarn for the G&M Railway was directly behind the theater, and when the trolleys pulled in for the night, the theater would rumble and shake like an earthquake. The 600-seat theater continued to show movies until 1987, when it burned down. The site is now the parking lot for Andersen's.

This sign welcomed shoppers in the 1920s and 1930s. Designed and home-built by a group of merchants, the sign was made of a log, cut flat on one side, with electric lights inserted in it to spell out Montrose and hung across Honolulu Avenue at the western side of the Montrose Hotel. Today a cement sign built on the curb at Honolulu Avenue and Verdugo Road greets visitors.

The Valley Pharmacy (shown in the early 1930s) was built on the northwest corner of Ocean View Boulevard and Honolulu Avenue in 1926. It was the classic pharmacy of that era, which often included a soda fountain and ice cream bar. The decorative brick facade was covered with stucco after the Sylmar earthquake. In 2008, the owner considered restoring the brick facade, but the underlying damage to the bricks made it cost prohibitive.

This two-level, single-story brick building on the west side of Ocean View Boulevard north of Honolulu Avenue was built in the 1920s to house the Los Angeles County Sheriff's Department. The department moved to new quarters in the early 1970s, and businesses have operated in this building since, including Jailhouse Jean's, which used the jail cells as changing rooms. Once again, the intricate brick work was stuccoed over after the Sylmar quake.

In 1940, the Shopping Bag moved from its mom-and-pop-size market in Montrose to a larger store a few doors down. Shown here on opening night, complete with banners and floodlights, the building had some wonderful neon signs and accents. Typical of large Shopping Bag stores is the tall sign structure on the left. And typical of urban markets at the time is that it is completely open to the sidewalk. The tall sign structure is still there, hidden by trees.

For thousands of years, this oak-filled canyon was possibly the only spot in the valley that had close to year-round water. Tongva Indians made their home here until chased out by Spanish settlers in the late 1700s. In 1929, Charles Bowden turned it into a recreational spot, with a large swimming pool, snack bar, picnic grounds, and outdoor dance floor. The entrance was on Verdugo Road, east of the business district of Montrose. Drivers passed through an arch (next page) and descended down into the canyon.

Bowden named his park Indian Springs and built it using a Southwest/American Indian theme. The property changed hands several times but steadily provided a welcome relief from heat for residents of Crescenta Valley from 1929 until 1966, when the pool developed a large crack. Instead of fixing it, the new owner filled in not only the pool but also the entire canyon with dirt removed from the future site of Verdugo Hills Hospital up the street. The shopping center has recently been remodeled.

Here is the grand opening of Fitzsimmons Market, located on Verdugo Road just south of Honolulu Avenue, probably in the early 1940s. To attract attention, the promoters decorated the store with patriotic bunting and brought in floodlights for the evening show: a trapeze act, not unlike the acrobat shows the Beverly Center put on to bring in customers. It is not known when Fitzsimmons was torn down, but Cavalier Hair Salon and Sun Palace Chinese restaurant are there now.

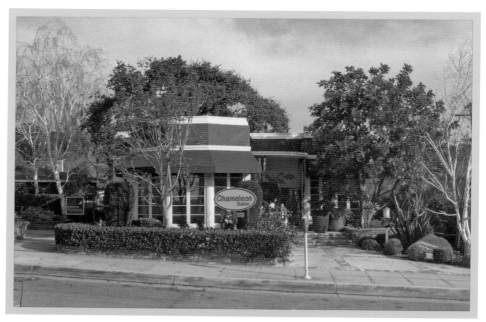

Dr. Robert Longman opened his dentist office in Montrose on the second floor of the Reinhardt Building in the booming 1920s. Despite the Great Depression that had crippled the country, Dr. Longman had done well enough by 1938 to build his own offices at 2039 Montrose Avenue. That building now houses Chameleon Beauty Salon and is the front end of a complex of charming cottage offices and residences, including the small cabins that were once the Montrose Motel, an old motor court–style motel.

The Zwick family lived in a little house in the 2300 block of Honolulu Avenue from the 1920s, when it was a residential area, into the 1970s, after it had become part of the Montrose Shopping Park. In this photograph from the 1950s, it is the small house in front. In the 1970s, family friend John Bluff bought the house and replaced it with an office and shopping complex, naming it Zwick's Plaza. He also preserved the handprints the Zwick sons had left in cement when very young.

In an effort to save the financial district, local business owners formed the Montrose Shopping Park Association in 1967 and took the bold move of rebuilding the Montrose business district, removing some street parking, building out the curbs to make a winding road, and planting trees and shrubs to give the area a more park-like setting. This newspaper photograph from June 1967 shows the new curbing being finished at Honolulu and Ocean View for the soon-to-open Montrose Shopping Park.

CHAPTER 3

GLENDALE

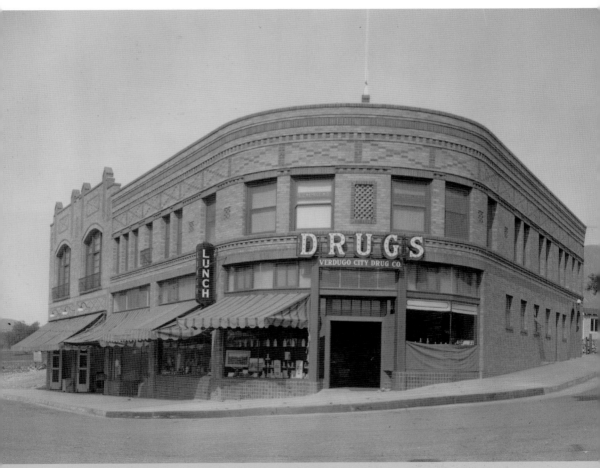

Before the Glendale annexation in 1951, the valley included several named neighborhoods. One of them was Verdugo City, developed in 1925 by Harry Fowler around the intersection of La Crescenta and Honolulu Avenues. At the centerpiece of Verdugo City (on the northwest corner) was this spectacular brick building, which featured a drugstore with a soda fountain and lunch counter, several storefronts, and a community auditorium on the second floor.

For years, the Verdugo City centerpiece was occupied by Roger's Pharmacy and Trade Rite Market, which was owned by Bill Bailey, one of the founders of the local Rotary Club and responsible for many improvements in the valley. The 1971 Sylmar earthquake damaged this beautiful building beyond repair, and it was replaced with a gas station. In the now photograph, Art Cobery stands where he once worked as a box boy in the Trade Rite Market during World War II.

In 1912, the main route to the valley from Los Angeles was the unpaved Verdugo Road, shown here where Mountain Street now intersects it. This photograph was probably taken from the horse-drawn wagon of the Fallin Stage Line, which ran regularly from downtown Los Angeles to the valley. On the left are the tracks of what would become the Glendale and Montrose Railway. Verdugo Road has been paved and significantly widened, but it has been replaced as the main route by the Frank Lanterman (2) Freeway.

A bridge over Verdugo Creek at the southern end of the Verdugo Canyon was first built for the electric trolleys that brought visitors to Montrose. The 1934 flood destroyed that bridge. It was rebuilt by WPA workers only to be washed out again in the 1938 flood, as seen in this photograph. Because this was the major entry point to Crescenta Valley, the bridge was immediately rebuilt, this time by the Army Corps of Engineers. The same bridge stands today.

This wide median on Verdugo Road, south of Montrose, was the track bed of the Glendale and Montrose Railway. Soon after G&M went out of business, the rails were removed for scrap, and the wooden ties were cut up as firewood for the needy of La Crescenta. Local residents moved trees from their own yards to beautify the median. The then photograph was taken in the 1940s.

In the early 1900s, William Sparr, then the largest fruit grower in California, planted citrus orchards on his acreage in the lower portion of the Crescenta Valley. During the land boom of the 1920s, Sparr decided his land was worth more than his fruit and ripped out most of his trees. He subdivided his property in 1922 and eventually named it Sparr Heights. His real estate office was donated to Glendale and is now the Sparr Heights Community Center.

In the Roaring Twenties, the small community of Highway Highlands was laid out on the undeveloped sagebrush land along State Highway 118 (now Foothill Boulevard) between Dunsmore and Boston Avenues. Shown here is the 3600 block in the 1940s. Apparently expecting a big future, the developers numbered the streets—First Avenue all the way to Fifth Avenue. Highway Highlands was part of the Glendale annex in 1951, but residents today sometimes refer to their neighborhood as "The Avenues."

This was the intersection of Foothill Boulevard and Pennsylvania Avenue looking west in the late 1930s. Known as State Highway 118 at the time, it was a fairly quiet road with few businesses, as most of the surrounding land was orchards and vineyards stretching from La Cañada to Tujunga. Note the sign directing visitors to the Ananda Ashrama, a religious retreat that was then well known (and still exists). This intersection today marks the border of Glendale and unincorporated La Crescenta.

Thirty-three acres on the northern edge of the Verdugos were transformed from a speakeasy and surrounding woodlands to Mountain Oaks Resort in 1929. The private club had many recreational facilities, including a lodge (formerly the speakeasy), riding stables, ball fields, trout ponds, and this swimming pool, known as Crystal Pool, which was occasionally opened to the community. Mountain Oaks went out of business in the 1960s, but the abandoned pool still stands, fairly intact in the wooded area.

GLENDALE

In the middle decades of the last century, La Crescenta resident George Wadey owned a gas station on the southwest corner of Pennsylvania and Honolulu Avenues, which was then on the main route to Tujunga. Wadey collected foreign and antique cars. He is shown here in the late 1930s driving past his gas station in a Fiat race car once owned by racing pioneer Barney Oldfield. The building still stands.

In 1946, Milton Hofert bought what had been the Mount Lukens Tubercular Sanitarium and its 10-acre grounds. Hofert was an avid collector of junk, and for 10 years, he built stone walls all over the property, embedding them with a jumble of found objects like car parts, wagon wheels, and kitchen utensils. In 1957, when the City of Glendale bought the property that would become Dunsmore Park, Hofert insisted that his folk art walls be preserved.

The valley had its own wacky merchant in the person of Fred Rebal, who, in 1946, opened Rebal's Mad House "where a fast nickel beats a slow dime." He billed his full-service market at 2931 Honolulu Avenue as the store "that made Verdugo City famous" and offered occasional pony rides in the parking lot. He advertised, "It's fun to shop at Rebal's Mad House! Have you had your fun today?" Other markets have occupied this building since then but none as fun.

To sell the new homes built in the valley in the boom after World War II, tiny real estate offices lined Foothill Boulevard, each trying to do something unique to draw attention. Ruth Powell's Real Estate at 3541 Foothill Boulevard contained elements typical of the 1960s (when this photograph was taken), including the zigzag roofline with the hanging lamps under the eaves and the lava rock facade foundation. Many of the tiny buildings on Foothill Boulevard were at one time real estate offices.

Peter Prescott, an Italian immigrant, established a lumber business in La Cañada in 1923. When postwar building in the valley boomed, Prescott opened a second store in 1949 at 3522 Foothill Boulevard in La Crescenta. Foothill Lumber was passed down to Pete Prescott Jr. in 1959. It changed hands several times after that until finally going out of business in 2008. The new owner caused a stir in the community with plans to build a three-story office building on the site.

The 1940s and 1950s were boom years for growth in the Crescenta Valley. The hotels and motels that had catered to health seekers and tourists for the previous 50 years were now being used as much for temporary housing as for overnight stays, as newcomers lived in places like the Valley Motel (above) while house hunting. This motel, located on Honolulu Avenue near Orangedale Avenue, a block west of the Montrose business district, was demolished in the early 1980s.

Many different buildings have occupied the northeast corner of Broadview Drive and Verdugo Road since the development of Montrose, including a small real estate office in the teens and a service station from 1960s to 2007. This photograph from the late 1970s shows it when it was a Standard station. Recently a large medical office building was erected on the site. The size and style generated many complaints from residents who felt that the building was designed without proper community input.

The Le Mesnager family built this stone barn in 1914 as a home and a winery to serve their extensive vineyards in the valley. Wildfires burned the barn in 1933 (below), creating a river of wine as 20,000 gallons burst from burning wooden barrels. A river of mud and debris struck weeks later in the New Year's Flood. The Le Mesnager family rebuilt the barn and lived here for another 30 years. It is now the centerpiece of Deukmejian Wilderness Park.

Rockhaven Sanitarium was established in 1923 by a young nurse as a safe haven for women with mental illnesses. It grew over the years and, by the 1950s, featured this gated entrance and natural stone wall. A 1964 street widening project took out the wall, and a truck knocked down the arch, which was then welded to the gate. Rockhaven was the last of what was once the major industry (sanitarium-style health facilities) of the valley. Glendale purchased the property in 2008 for use as a library and community center.

CHAPTER 4

LA CAÑADA

La Cañada was primarily a farming community during its early years, but in 1892, a harbinger of the wealthy suburb it would become was constructed high up on what is now Ocean View Boulevard: the Gould Castle. Built by Eugene and May Gould, the castle overlooked the Crescenta Valley and was the site of lavish parties attended by the Los Angeles elite. Tourists enjoyed the spectacle of the guests in their finery riding to the castle in their horse-drawn carriages.

Modeling the castle after one she had seen in Spain, May Gould spared no expense in its construction, importing marble columns from Europe and having huge granite blocks hauled up from the valley floor. A risky business strategy cost the Goulds their fortune, and since few others could afford the upkeep, the castle was abandoned for decades and finally torn down in the 1950s. Shown above just before demolition, the tree in front looks nearly the same today.

Inspired by the Goulds, Lt. Gov. Albert Wallace built his own castle nearby, but Mrs. Wallace felt pre-Flintridge La Cañada was too much a farming community for her taste, so they sold it in 1914. The new owner spent a few too many weeks away from his new bride, and in anger, she painted the castle pink. Like the Gould castle, the pink castle was abandoned for a while, but in the 1990s, the castle was renovated and reinhabited.

When Michigan Avenue (now Foothill Boulevard) was first laid out as a straight road by Edward Haskell in the late 1800s, it had to traverse many canyons and gullies. To smooth the wagon rides, wooden trestles were built, the largest being at Hilliard Avenue in La Cañada. In 1901, the ravines were filled by dumping dirt off the bridge from wagons, until the fill reached the level of the bridge roadway. Today this intersection is where 2 Freeway meets Foothill Boulevard.

The beginnings of a church for the new community of La Cañada started with informal services at the home of Jacob and Ammoretta Lanterman, who then donated a parcel of land. The first church was built in 1898, and the current one replaced that in 1924. A year later, a dramatic backlit stained-glass window was added, leading California's state poet laureate, John Steven McGroarty, to immortalize it as the "Church of the Lighted Window." In 1969, the church was declared a California State Historic Landmark.

In the 1910s, former senator Frank Flint bought 1,700 acres of land on the southern side of the valley and developed it with streets, utilities, horse trails, a country club, golf course, and riding stables, naming the area after himself. Sales offices were set up throughout Flintridge, and this particular tract office, located on a lot on the northwest corner of Berkshire and Commonwealth Avenues, seemed to be doing a brisk business, but apparently could not sell that very lot, which mysteriously sits empty today.

Alta Canyada Road was originally the driveway for the Barnum Ranch, and the palm trees lining the drive were planted in 1891 by the Barnum family. This photograph, taken in 1914 just above Foothill Boulevard, shows young Willard Barnum in a horse-and-buggy rig. Many palms on the eastern side have been removed, but most of the western row remains. The Barnum family lived on Fairview near the top of Alta Canyada for decades.

In 1914, Jim Huntington, on the right, stands across Michigan Avenue (Foothill Boulevard) from the blacksmith shop where he embarked on a career in metalwork that brought him nationwide fame. His metalwork in the form of iron gates and fences was in demand all over Los Angeles and can be seen locally at St. Francis High School and Rockhaven Sanitarium. An innovator and inventor, he is widely credited with creating the first portable barbecue in 1939. His former shop still stands.

In the early 1880s, Col. Tom Hall, a Civil War veteran, homesteaded 1,000 acres on the north side of the valley, just east of Pickens Canyon. He planted extensive vineyards and was soon producing barrels of wine like the one seen in this photograph. The Halls sold much of the homestead in 1912 to developer E. T. Earl, who laid out the curving streets of Alta Canyada and replaced the grapevines with deodar trees, but the old barn survives.

This was the Arroyo Seco Fire Protection Division Headquarters in 1936 at the intersection of Foothill Boulevard and Georgian Road in La Cañada. The county took over fire protection duties for Crescenta-Cañada in the early 1920s. Before that, volunteers did firefighting with shovels, buckets, and wet gunnysacks. This is that same stone structure at 352 N. Foothill Boulevard, now incorporated into the larger building that has been built around it.

Early valley businesses often gave to the community by providing facilities for public services, realizing that their profitability was directly tied to the health and well-being of the community. In the late 1930s, Wynn-Norton Realty built a beautiful new office in La Cañada and turned over half of the building for use as a new U.S. Post Office. Located on Foothill Boulevard, one block west of Angeles Crest Highway, the building has hardly changed.

Ranked number one on the American Film Institute's "100 Years . . . 100 Cheers" list, the 1946 Frank Capra movie *It's A Wonderful Life* was partly filmed in a new housing tract in the fast growing (but not yet incorporated) suburb of La Cañada. This is at Viro Road and Lamour Drive. Today it is hard to recognize the spot because of the vegetation. There is a tree in about the same location as the one in the film, but that tree was a special effect.

In the film, Jimmy Stewart portrays George Bailey, who asks "is it too much to have them [the locals] live and die in a couple of rooms and a bath?" He builds Bailey Park, and here, George welcomes the Martini family to their new home. While two rooms and a bath were enough in 1946, "McMansions" have replaced many of the 1940s bungalows. However the Martini house looks almost unchanged, perhaps because of its connection to one of the most beloved movies of all time.

In 1953, the land on the north side of Foothill Boulevard, just east of Castle Road, was leveled for the construction of La Cañada Village Shopping Center. Before any building was started, a huge circus tent was set up on the land, and a five-day Crescenta Valley Community Fair was held. Ralph's opened later that year and was a valley fixture for four decades before moving to the old Kimball Sanitarium site in the 1990s. The former Ralph's is now a Ross.

In 1959, Norbert and Irene Olberz, new immigrants to the United States, bought a small ski shop and named it Sport Chalet. In 1974, they bought the old Shopping Bag building and opened the first full-size Sport Chalet. After years of negotiations, Olberz's dream of a La Cañada Town Center opened in 2008, with the HomeGoods store standing where the original Sport Chalet stood. The new Sport Chalet is on the back side of the town center.

In 1955, there were 24 air raid sirens intended to warn citizens of an eminent Russian attack. The sirens were installed in the Los Angeles area, including this one in the San Rafael Mountains above Glendale and the Crescenta/Cañada Valley. With a decibel level of 138 and an effective range of 4 miles, this siren blared at 10:00 a.m. on the last Friday of every month in air raid drills for 20-some years. It's still there but hasn't been sounded in decades.

The first bridge across the Arroyo Seco was opened in May 1893, making the important connection between Pasadena and the Crescenta/Cañada Valley. In this photograph, residents celebrated the opening in the shade of the arroyo. The bridge has been replaced over the years, first by the roadway on top of the dam, then by the bridge that is now Oak Grove Drive, and finally by the 210 Freeway. But the old pilings are still there, just inside Devil's Gate Dam.

On October 17, 1972, a large section of the Arroyo Seco Bridge portion of the 210 Freeway collapsed during construction. While cement was being poured, 150 feet of forms, scaffolding, and wet cement suddenly fell 90 feet into the streambed of the Arroyo Seco. Six workers were killed and another 21 injured. It took 18 hours to extricate the dead and injured from under tons of wood, steel, and cement debris. By August 1974, this section of the freeway finally opened for traffic.

By the early 1970s, after decades of fighting and negotiation between the community and the state, the 210 Freeway cut through the heart of the Crescenta Valley. This photograph from 1972 looks south at the growing 2/210 interchange being built over Verdugo Road near the Montrose–La Cañada border. The land under this interchange was initially developed as a Ford dealership, but it was replaced by a movie theater in the late 1990s.

www.arcadiapublishing.com

Discover books about the town where you grew up, the cities where your friends and families live, the town where your parents met, or even that retirement spot you've been dreaming about. Our Web site provides history lovers with exclusive deals, advanced notification about new titles, e-mail alerts of author events, and much more.

Arcadia Publishing, the leading local history publisher in the United States, is committed to making history accessible and meaningful through publishing books that celebrate and preserve the heritage of America's people and places. Consistent with our mission to preserve history on a local level, this book was printed in South Carolina on American-made paper and manufactured entirely in the United States.

This book carries the accredited Forest Stewardship Council (FSC) label and is printed on 100 percent FSC-certified paper. Products carrying the FSC label are independently certified to assure consumers that they come from forests that are managed to meet the social, economic, and ecological needs of present and future generations.

Find *Your* Place in History.